ONE
OF
A
KIND

SUSHIL THIND

Michael Terence
Publishing

First published in paperback by
Michael Terence Publishing in 2019
http://mtp.agency

ISBN 9781913289478

Sushil Thind has asserted the right to be identified as the
author of this work in accordance with the
Copyright, Designs and Patents Act 1988

Copyright © 2019 Sushil Thind

All rights reserved. No part of this publication may be reproduced,
stored in a retrieval system, or transmitted, in any form or by any
means, electronic, mechanical, photocopying, recording or
otherwise, without the prior permission of the publishers

Cover images
Copyright © Maritime

Cover design
Copyright © 2019 Michael Terence Publishing

Dedicated in memory of Sham lal Thind & Reshma Devi…

Contents

The Way I Feel 1

Brotherly Love 3

Helpful Hand 5

Mother 7

Bright Outcome 9

Look At Me Now 11

Beloved Brother 13

Love 15

What Am I? 17

Holidays 19

Beloved Mother 21

Dad 23

You're In My Face 25

You Was Here 27

Our Family 29

Exams, Exams 31

You Once Again 33

The Way I Feel

The way I am feeling is not the same every day,
Come so far,
Yet I'm so lost
Remember feelings that I had forgot,
Sometimes feel so good, then feel the pain,
The inner pain which cannot be explained.

Above all that I was strong,
The happiness to me I thought belonged,
Unfortunately I was so wrong.

In my own way loud and bubbly.
I used to be.

Brotherly Love

The day I forget my brother
Is the day I will be another
The day you left here
From that day all I felt is fear.
Then I think to myself, you're still near
Brother I wish you was still here forever.

I will always pray for you
A promise which is true
You'll always remain in my heart and that never apart
The time comes for all to move on.

Life is like a game
We all take day by day
One day you can be in fame, next you can dwell in so much pain.

Helpful Hand

The pain that I am feeling and going through
I honestly don't know what to do
Someone who would listen
And understand how I feel.

Someone who would care to be a listening ear,
For when I'm in most fear,
Someone who would put my pain at ease
Just by talking to me.

Mother

Remember the times you held me close and felt safe and protected,
The times when I may have crossed the line,
So easily you used to forgive,
Everything then used to be fine.

So many years it has been now
That you've gone,
Cannot believe it's been so long,
You'll always be in my heart,
And never far apart,
You was my mother, best friend and sister
I dearly do miss you.

Bright Outcome

You came into my life and made it bright,
Angry with you long I could not be,
Odd few occasions,
Together we still are,
And not far apart,
Day by day we're getting stronger,
And together for longer,
My heart still skips a beat,
Every time we meet.

There's many hating
Them we do defeat, as if we've known each other for many years
When I'm with you I feel no fear.

Beautiful colours, Red is for wine,
Blue to be mine,
Green is for energy and to feel free,
Yellow because of the hot summers,
When it's funnier,
Brown please don't feel down,
Orange for the sunset,

Gold be bright and for those who are loud,
To be proud,
Silver to be a winner,
Pink soft makes you think sweet,
Purple for the twinkle tulips
Makes me think of music
Cream

Look At Me Now

Look at me now
You said I was a nobody
But now I am someone
Now that you've gone
I've learnt to live and crack a smile
Though you used to call me ugly and vile.

Used me for my money
Oh no honey
No more!
Because you're not funny…

Beloved Brother

Sitting and wondering
Who knows how I feel?

Missing my brother again and again,
Wondering if I will see him and when?
Pain that I go through day and night,
Wondering if I will see him again…

People say let go,
How do I let go?
Whatever happened to this one?
As for now and forever he has gone…

Wherever you are brother of mine
I hope you're fine
Now and forever you'll always remain that same brother of mine.

Love

The feelings I have for you
Are deep
When I think of you
I cannot sleep

When someone wrongly mentions our names
They have nothing better to talk about
What a shame
Together we will remain

As long as we're together they will be no end
A message to everyone I will send

What Am I?

It's so cold and sweet,
Melts so softly in your mouth
Oh watch!
Don't get it on the couch,
Or else mother will shout,
Look!
There's an ice cream van outside the house
The children quickly running towards it no doubt,
Different flavours which are savers
Loads of choices …
I want this one from all these little voices.

Holidays

Holidays holidays here again,
Lots of activities for children to do,
Parents what would we do?
Loads of money spent,
Hearing...
I'm tired, I'm hungry, I'm bored!
Thank God it's only for a week,
So I do not fear
I dread it as soon the six weeks holidays are near.

Beloved Mother

Forget you mother,
I will not!
Miss you mom without a doubt,
No matter how many attempts that are taken
God you did very wrong on that day,
My mom you did take
The biggest mistake
You did make

So lonely and sad since you have gone…

Dad

Still remember the times when I needed you the most
You was always there
When I was down
You automatically knew

Parents are mind readers
So so true!
You was a helper
Cherished our good times
You was the strength which could not be broken
Celebrations which are not the same without you
All I feel is…

Sadness and pain

You're In My Face

You're in my face at all times
Because you think to do so
It's fine
Moan and moan again,
Is all do you,
We are so glad we're through
It was the last thing I wanted to do,
Is to stay with you.

Now go and take a break,
Learn to love yourself
Or get some form of help!

You Was Here

One day you was here
Then you passed and now I wish you was here
I miss you so much,
Dad!
Because it hits me so much now that your no longer here.

All I do is feel fear,
And wish you was here!

Our Family

My children,
You four will always be…

One, two, three and four and then me,
To lie to each other we shall not.

As a strong tie with a knot,
Shall not be forgotten,
I will always love you all with my heart.

Exams, Exams

Exams, exams
A frightening time,
But guess what?
You'll be fine!
Rise and revise and be in school on time

Missing out on lessons,
Is a big not to do!
Otherwise next lesson you'll have no clue,
Of what to do…

Whatever you take on, and want to be,
As you'll get older you'll see,
So don't ignore…
Listen to me!

You Once Again

Think of you once again,
Don't know which way to turn,
My heart for you will always burn,
Why and where did I go wrong?

Twenty-four seven I think of you,
Remembering the times it was us two,
To forget you I have tried,
To myself I have lied,
Once I told you I will wait.

Now I wait for that date…

*Available worldwide from
Amazon and all good bookstores*

―――――――

http://mtp.agency

http://facebook.com/mtp.agency

@mtp_agency

www.ingramcontent.com/pod-product-compliance
Lightning Source LLC
LaVergne TN
LVHW020446080526
838202LV00055B/5360